Stones for Sanity

*Prison humor
from an old jail guard.*

http://stones-for-sanity.ronnagy.net

Introduction

For most jail is not a pleasant experience. The incarcerated especially for the younger offender is a wake up call. I'm not writing about the State or Federal systems-Hard Time. I'm writing about the first stop-the County jail system. Possibly the first time offender will learn his/her lesson-30% or more will eventually graduate to the state or Federal-hard time experience. Can we change this?

The first time kids-the kids I'm writing about the majority came from broken homes, they slipped through the system-kids that were ADHD, Bi-Polar, Hyperthymic and a mirage of psychological conditions that are being masked over by using alcohol, illegal drugs and acting out their frustrations-the self medicating syndrome. Our society has failed miserably.

I was drawn into corrections not by a good paycheck or a relatively secure job. I was drawn to corrections by the feeling I could make a difference, influence lives that had gone awry. Societies mentality of "locking up and throwing away the key" is not the answer for "correction". Correction without instilling positive self-esteem, basic living skills and job skills is useless. Hundreds of millions of dollars are being used to build Institutions of wire and walls. These millions should be used at an earlier age by trained health care professionals in our school systems by recognizing the "troubled youth"-they are our future. They are reaching out and we must be aware and HELP.

Some are so wounded and they bury those wounds deep. It is our responsibility to discern-not condemn. Humor is healing, and listening can also heal. My approach to pain was to use humor-not everyone will agree with me but humor was my way to mask pain. My pain is when I failed-not everyone can be helped. That is the pain I live with today.

Stones for Sanity

Stones have meaning for each of us. Cemetery Stones and monuments, stone farm field walls and picking stones from a garden area. Skipping stones, dropping a stone in a lake and watching the disturbance cause ring upon ring until it spreads so far it becomes invisible.

Mourners in a cemetery place stones upon each other in a meditative state of consciousness saying prayers for the one who passed on. Frustrations can be released by hammering stones smaller and smaller. Heaving and throwing stones for exercise can release pent-up frustrations.

I always carry small stones of various shapes and colors in my pockets to touch and roll in my hands as a thinking process or to relax a mental situation-a nervous habit. Everyone has his or her way of staying centered and sane.

In the Prison Farm Program there were nervous days, nervous days for both the Officers and the Inmates. Whether it was the Moon Phase or lousy weather-nervous energy had to be channeled in a positive way. No one wanted thirty guys and two Officers bound with nervous energy. On 150 acres of farm land, hills, valleys or cultivated areas there were a lot of stones.

I never used the word ROCKS. The word rocks seemed like work. A day of picking and throwing stones or filling wheelbarrows was used as a positive release of pent up nervous energy. Extraordinary stones were found and sometimes Indian Arrowheads. The Arrowheads were bagged and were taken home by the person who discovered one. An arrowhead was a real prize to show the family back home.

We had contests of who could throw a same size stone the greater distance. Wheelbarrows were filled and dumped over the sides of a hill to watch how far they could roll. Stone-picking day was looked forward to. Most Inmates thought I was NUTS-but the stones idea worked. Stones became a natural medicine for nervous energy, frustrations, pent up energy and kept the "Blue's" away. This is why I call my collection of short stories Stones For Sanity.

Nagster

Contents

Terror on the Wall

There were good days and not so good. The Old Jail was built around the end of the 19th Century. Damp, dark with heavy stonewalls, flat Iron strap bars, small overcrowded cells. Multiple tiers of cells were in the back jail and a lower and upper level front jail for special medical classifications. This is the kind of jail you pay for now. Ghost tours costing ten dollars or more to get scared when someone jumps out at you. Don't forget to take pictures of ORBS. This jail was a classic.

A rookie, I worked 2nd shift. My first night I came in the front door and the heavy six-inch thick door thumped loud behind me-possibly deliberately. I got the message. I walked through 2 sets of "sally ports"-sally ports were two heavy sets of bars-cages separated six feet apart. No two gates would be opened at one time-security was good.

You walked through the front jail all Ironed, pressed and spiffed up looking good for the shift change and roll call. The first day I got chocolate pudding-or what I hoped was chocolate pudding. At least it smelled like pudding. Some days you got covered with pudding-some days Jell-O or if you were really liked both chocolate pudding and Jell-O mixed. Second tier Inmates waited and this was their special time of day-shift change fun.

Each night was a new experience-a different duty area

9

every night. I was going to learn every aspect of the jail and how to handle any situation. I made my way around. Three men in each small cell and hopefully they all got along. If not there was a fight to stop. Recreation was special in the back jail. Two hours of in the back jail freedom and mayhem for us. I survived; I made my "bones". Everyday I prayed for 11pm and the front door was finally my freedom.

One evening I had outside Wall duty. Considered a gravy job with fresh air and quiet. I was assigned a police 870-pump shotgun and a 38 Remington pistol. I was escorted to the outside and to the enclosed Wall entrance stairs with 14 steps up and locked from the outside. I had no key and would be relieved by the next shift. Five O'clock, six o'clock and coffee was delivered. I lowered a thin rope and bucket over the inside wall and I pulled up a fresh hot container of coffee. I had it good.

By seven o'clock a heavy fog started forming and a heavy mist covered everything. I radioed in my usual 15-minute radio checks-heavy fog and zero visibility, nothing unusual, all secure. Keep pacing the wall-look to my right, look to my left no one breaks in and no one breaks out. The Presbyterian Church and Graveyard was to my left and back. I knew the dead could not hurt me but the cemetery bothered me. Something caused me to take a quick extra look to my left-toward the cemetery. Forty feet away I spotted a white glob forming behind one of the larger tombstones and growing larger. A chill went down my spine. I didn't believe in Ghosts I was too rational. BUT I had never experienced one.

I clicked the safety off both the 38 and the 870 shotgun. The 870 came off my shoulder where a strap secured it. I'm now at the terrified pee your pants stage. Can I shoot a Ghost? I wasn't watching the jail any longer-the ghost had my attention. Higher, whiter and larger should I use the shot-gun first, I couldn't miss with the shotgun spread. The 45 had to be a direct hit. The 870 was my best chance especially in the fog.

I leveled the 870 and aimed. A firearm blast from the wall would cause complete turmoil in the jail and a lot of paperwork. Should I call it in? How do you radio in you see a Ghost? That would be just as bad as calling in a UFO. I'd never live through all the teasing I'd get from that. Even if a UFO was spotted-keep it quiet or the shrink has his turn with you. Every officer in the jail was on the same radio frequen-cy-they would think I lost my mind. Decisions under duress and fear are difficult. You are only thinking about ME first.

Shotgun leveled and was ready to fire then I heard a loud BELCH BURP echo through the fog. O my God. The church had a Wedding and Reception party today. The "Ghost" didn't make it home. She was a large woman wearing a white dress and passed out in the cemetery-behind a tomb stone. My eyes met hers and a nasty exchange of words mostly from the wall brought on another BELCH BURP from the "GHOST WOMAN".

Fernando and the "Farm Louse"

Fernando received a jail sentence—he broke the law-he was caught. Fernando was not a bad kid-he was just so gullible and he wanted so much to fit in with the buddies he acquired from the "streets". Many of Fernando's friends were not caught just as many others are not caught-but Fernando was somewhat slow with a low IQ. Fernando was a likable guy and I felt he held promise and he could be helped and rehabilitated.

When Fernando first came into jail I had already been told he would be coming and would I try and help him. Of course that was my purpose to help those who could be helped and make hell to the one's who would not want help. Some called me Nagster some called me the Devil himself-I preferred the previous. Fernando had some hard lessons to learn. First was the separation from family and friends and 2nd was trust and respect for Authority. Fernando was removed from the main Prison system and was placed in our Farm Program.

The Farm was an outside the walls work program where he would live in the farmhouse. The Farm was a place where he could learn basic living skills along with life's positive interaction with his fellow men and go out on an assigned farm property detail each day. It was one of my jobs to train these mostly city kids on the proper use of lawn equipment, shovels, basic farm tools axes and so on. This sounds odd to someone who has spent most of their lives living in the suburbs and country. But these were "city cement jungle" kids. There is a difference between city kids and country kids. Especially convicted offenders who I prefer to think of as delinquents not incarcerated inmates.

These individuals ranged from 18 yr. olds to the early 40's. A psychiatrist would not officially classify them as "older delinquents". But I felt that way. The longer I took to hand out sets of the regulation orange outside wear farm uniforms the more I realized that Fernando was not just slow but more than slow and very timid and scared. Fernando would take much more patience than I ever realized. This is how it started out with Fernando. He was one of the most trying guys of my career. There were 30 total "delinquents" housed at the farmhouse and along with several other round the clock officers we had near complete control of this program.

A 200 year old stone farm house several hundred yards from the main institution separated by a corn field and heavy over grown brush gave us almost a complete separation from the inside walls and much worse conditions. As I said Fernando was a special case. The other guys would definitely take advantage of Fernando. He was exceptionally gullible, an 18yr old kid trapped in a man's body. It was Monday morning when chore day started. As I gave out assignments and tools for those jobs Fernando stood just watching. He did not know the difference between a flat and pointed shovel and an axe from a hatchet. This could really be tough. It would take much longer to explain a job to Fernando then the time it would take him to comprehend. Fernando was also scarred to death of the mower engine noise and possible imminent danger.

A bright idea crossed my mind. I needed a laundry man since the laundry man was recently discharged. Could Fernando do the laundry job? I would have him near the house and could check up on him often. Anyone could do laundry so I thought. I'll mention just one instance of instructing, explaining and demonstrating. Separating Fernando would be much easier than supervising 29 other delinquents along with Fernando.

Two Maytag Washers, two Maytag Dryers, six rooms of laundry two baskets for each room. One basket for color clothes and one for white should be no problem? I explained how each day an assigned man from each room would bring the laundry to the basement utility room and at the end of the workday the same man returned to carry the same baskets to his room. Easy? I'm explaining the various knobs and gadgets on the machines and the reason to use each one. I said wash one room at a time-don't mix the colors with the whites. Fernando was a light complected Spanish African American. I had absolutely no idea what I had said meant to Fernando's street intelligence.

I explained what I thought was needed to know about doing such a simple chore as "house laundry". I explained timing, folding, amount of laundry powder and so on. I realized I had made a mistake. I forgot to show how him where the water shut off valves were. Before I left I repeated not to wash the colors with the whites.

I was gone only a little over an hour when Kenny one of the cooks came running down the hill holding out two hands before him and said Fernando is having a "little problem" with the laundry. Kenny was holding globs of bubbles of which he was quite amused.

I got to the cellar door way, opened the door and it was bubble wonderland. Bubbles a foot deep along with inches of water were covering the entire basement. Fernando was standing on top of one of the Maytag washers forcing all color clothes into one washer, water running and the soap was all ready sprinkled. OH My God why me—OH my God, Fernando must have weighed a hundred pounds wet and he was wet-so was I. Bubble and water wet. Fernando said officer Nagster you told me not to wash the colors with the white and there are more colors than white people in this room. Kenny was watching and said; No I don't want to remember what Kenny said. Kenny will have his day. I am going to find something real special for Kenny.

How could I ever get angry with Fernando-he was so gullible, so sincere and absolutely honest with me No I could not be angry with Fernando. But Kenny will have his day. The vengeance side of me-the "devil himself".

Now I knew of no uncertain doubt Fernando would need extra special attention. The guys were having too much fun with Fernando and inadvertently I was also being watched. I would not give up on Fernando. I'm sure Kenny got Fernando all mixed up-I may never know but just that 6th sense told me. There were now bubbles and Pink clothes and sheets instead of white. Fernando was ok for a week or so-maybe Kenny thought he better lay low for a while and good he did because I was now watching both a clown delinquent and just gullible Fernando.

About a week or so later Kenny took a loaf of fresh bread, grabbed it in the middle and tore a big hole in the loaf just as if a wild animal was prowling for food. He threw it outside the back Kitchen farm stairs on the walkway where Fernando had to walk to the utility room. I still had Fernando doing the Laundry. I would not give up on Fernando. I didn't get the name Nagster because I was real quick on the up-take-I had a heavy foot and a stiff elbow when I was driving. This bread routine went on a few days until I realized it was Kenny trying to scare Fernando again. I agreed and then Kenny let me in on the next prank. Or so I thought he did.

Fernando is now scared to "bejebers" and Kenny had Fernando walking to and from the laundry taping a spade shovel handle on the ground to scare this "Farm Louse" away. The Farm Louse is a wild animal bigger than a groundhog. Has longer and sharper teeth and can jump when startled and very unpredictable. Dam Kenny. Always up to something. Kenny says ah come on Nagster lets have a little fun-and again I agreed. Everyone is wondering why Fernando is carrying around a shovel. Kenny had a special way of keeping pranks quiet. At least who was behind the prank.

Each day Fernando became more scared to walk from the front door to the back basement each day. Kenny kept putting this torn bread outside the farm door and then he starting leaving wet prunes and spreading the breadcrumbs to the back farm root cellar door. Kenny said-Nagster-today is Fernando's day. Kenny explained the rest of his "Farm Louse" plan. Kenny disappeared and I got Fernando, with a broom handle this time and we slowly walked to the rear of the root cellar with Fernando tapping the handle. Breadcrumbs and raisons were everywhere. I said Fernando I think we had enough of this farm louse nuisance. We're going to get him away and out of here for good. The breadcrumbs led to the upper door of the two level root cellar. Two stories deep, damp, cold, dripping and dark. I had a flashlight and Fernando now almost beating the ground non-stop.

16

I had to hold Fernando's arm to assure him I was there and would protect him. My long heavy-duty flashlight was our only light. The farm louse was afraid of light. We were going to save the entire population of the farm from this farm louse today, just he and I. We had to go down those dark steps just he and I. The flashlight and broom handle were our only weapons. Fernando said: Nagster I really don't want to do this-don't make me do this. I said Fernando we are going to be Heroes!

Slowly, going down a step at a time at the bottom of the second section of steps my flashlight accidentally went dead. A hand grabbed my ankle. A wet sticky hand and something sharp like nails that felt like teeth. I let out a scream. Fernando was already running up the steps yelling for help. Kenny never told me I was the target at the end of the prank.

The next day I come to work and no Fernando. I asked where's Fernando? Kenny said Fernando went back to the main prison last evening and was admitted to a Psycho Ward. Dr. Bob the prison shrink telephoned me in the morning and asked: Nagster I have Fernando here and he says there is some kind of wild animal called a "Farm Louse" that attacked him yesterday-I said Dr. Bob I don't know of any wild animals over here-especially one called a "farm louse".

TINY

Tiny had a routine, a route he walked, or more like lumbered to every day. Tiny didn't use alcohol or drugs and he wasn't a salesman. Tiny's routine was frequenting several Donut shops downtown. Tiny always received a free Donut or two. He called this protection insurance for the Donut shop clerk.

Pricilla the new girl behind the counter didn't know about the "protection" routine. Today was Tiny's unlucky day. Tiny had a humorous and fun side to his personality except he could not keep a straight face He had the dry humor face that gets us all in trouble at times. Tiny pointed his finger back like a fat pistol and put 2 donuts on his finger and said this is a stick-up. A pun so he thought. Tiny was kidding. The cop hiding in the corner stuffing his face with his last jelly donut did not think this was funny. Pricilla was his girlfriend. Patrolman Andy called in a 10-10 in progress and asked for backup. Patrolman Andy was not going to handle a 6ft 2" 375lb crazed donut robber. Tiny got 9-23 months County time. Cops and Judges do not look upon Donut thefts very kindly.

The first time I met Tiny he was dressed all in white. The color uniform all main jail kitchen inmates wore. Two 3x uniforms had to be split in half and sewn together. Tiny was a big kid. Tiny didn't actually work in the kitchen. He sat on 4 milk crates stacked 2 high-8 crates. He watched and observed. Tiny was big. That's how Tiny got his nickname. Tiny came to jail with that nickname, it was a good nickname.

I was in the main jail kitchen to interview Tiny. An initial interview was required of all potential "farm" Inmate candidates. Tiny would be coming to the Farm. During the initial interview Tiny told me about his special job in the kitchen. I felt this special "watch and observe" position was mainly because if Tiny were to slip on the wet or damp floor he could fall upon someone and cause serious body harm to the one underneath.

Tiny didn't have any connections but his mother did and so did Jamal Tiny's older brother. Jamal was a Professional Football Line Backer, 6ft 5" 270 lbs. of pure muscle. We will hear more about Jamal later. The special request was from MOM for Tiny's best interests. MOM wanted to teach Tiny a lesson-learn responsibility, respect for authority and LOOSE WEIGHT. The Farm was an excellent choice. Through the grapevine MOM had heard about me the Nagster and the "Farm Program". Tiny was not a threat to society; he was just a big Donut Clown that caught a cop on a bad day. Arrangements had to be made before Tiny came to the Farm. Special orange uniforms would have to be split and sewn together. A special solid Iron regulation jail bed would have to be delivered. Farm beds were still like the military beds with spring bottoms. Heavy and wider Iron legged chairs to hold his weight and frame were made. The Farm never had such a large man.

The Farm Program was an outside the walls and wire work program where 30 men lived in a 3-story stone farm colonial house. Five upper rooms and 6 men in a room on bunk beds. Work was done on the 150 acres keeping the property in shape and generally looking good. This program also separated the hardcore Inmates from the newer less street wise dangerous Inmates. I call the Farm workers "societies Causalities" The guys that slipped through the cracks within our school systems and parents who were never able or aware of disorders such as ADHD, Bi-Polar etc. They were casualties.

Tiny was not going to sit on 8 milk crates and play "Jabba the Hut" on the Farm. Tiny was going to work just like everyone else. I had my job cut out for me. Dressed in orange with size 15 work boots on Tiny looked like a pumpkin with the roots still attached. The size pumpkin that would win the Season prize for largest and best. Tiny was a real easygoing kid. Nothing anyone would do or say to him could upset him. He had a real good sense of humor. Through the jail vine Tiny knew about the Nagsters frequent Donut raids. Tiny thought he would be in Donut Heaven".

After Tiny's 2nd day at the Farm I received so many complaints about his loud snoring we had to move Tiny into a spare clothes closet. The closet was same space as a regulation size jail cell. Tiny had his own room. Tiny didn't eat anymore than anyone else. He never ate a lot he just moved slower and on the streets lived on Donuts. Donuts were a special treat at the Farm, a reward. Tiny was not getting a regular Donut ration at the farm. I was trying to wean him off Donuts slowly. Mom's rule.

First visiting day came and Tiny's mom stopped in the office and she and I had a talk. Mom was only 5ft. 100lbs. But Tiny feared Mom. Mom had a lightning left hook and only hit the end of the nose. Tiny feared Mom more than any work job I would assign him to. MOM said NO Donuts take him off cold Turkey. During the visiting hour I heard a loud slam. Mom had stressed her point with her son. Tiny had complained to Mom about the Donut ration and the no snacks in the once a week Commissary delivery. Tiny never complained again. Tiny was afraid I would rat him out to MOM. I used this as leverage several times. I never had any problems with Tiny.

By the second week the no donut, no snacks and hard constant work Tiny had lost 25 lbs. was still not noticeable. We weighed Tiny on the Cattle Scale we had stored away in the Barn. Tiny painted, chopped wood, raked and cut grass. Tiny worked at his own pace and I always placed him where he could work at his own pace. 350 lbs. was a lot of kid to push too hard too fast and I'm not an EMT.

Anytime I gave Tiny a special job or an assignment he did not understand or confused him he could screw up his face in 10 different directions all at the same time as though he had no bones in his head. At the end of a month Tiny was down to 325lbs. Good, 50 lbs. Lost. Visiting Day MOM was pleased but said keep busting on him. At first I was trying to just get him in better shape. MOM was even tougher.

I felt he was ready for Plan B. Now, Plan B brought out the sinister part of me. Everyday before lunch I told Tiny to get into the Chevy Pick-up. We had a special job to do. We had to check the long road and the end of the hills to make sure all the Inmates had heard the Lunch Bell. Tiny always smiled getting into the Chevy Pick-up with me. He felt I had especially picked him for a special job over all the other guys. Tiny wasn't real quick. I mean sometimes Tiny's ego over powered his reasoning.

Each day I drove Tiny to the end of the road and around to the lower hills. I stopped the Pick-up. Tiny got out to have a look around. I said I had an important call in and had to run. Just walk back up the hill to the Farm Kitchen. After a couple of weeks of walking up a 3/4 mile long hill Tiny started to catch on. He would give me that screwed up in 10 different direction face look and all I had to do was whisper MOM. MOM was my secret weapon.

Tiny lost another 50 lbs. in the next 2 months. Tiny was getting in better shape-much better shape. He felt better about himself and generally was happier. He had withdrawn from Donuts and even stopped snoring so loud. No Inmate ever questioned me-that could be a disaster. Tiny never asked for a Donut and I never tempted him. I would sneak my Donut. I had my own donut habit.

The end of the 2nd Month Tiny was down to 300lbs. and more muscle was starting to appear. I was pleased. The Warden was out for a drive around one day when he spotted Tiny walking up the high hill all alone. The Warden came to the Farm House looking for me. He knew I was Tiny's "personal trainer". The Warden asked me if I was trying to Kill Tiny? I explained what my plan had been and what good results we were getting. The Warden said OK except from now on you walk up the hill with him. He did not want Tiny left alone just in case he should fall or whatever. Besides you look like you could use a few good walks yourself. Me having to walk the high hill ended Tiny's long walk training routine.

Furlough time arrived and Tiny's first weekend 2-day furlough arrived. Jamal picked up Tiny in his 4 door Dodge Pick-up Truck. Sunday night Tiny came back from furlough black and blue, limping. Tiny was not smiling. Jamal, Tiny's older Brother the Professional Football Linebacker had grabbed Tiny and threw him up 6 steps toward the second floor landing in Moms bi-level condo. This was just before moms lightning left hook could connect. Jamal was easy going most of the time. Jamal was home on season break.

I asked Tiny what had happened that he was so bruised and broken down. Tiny screwed up his face in the usual 10-direction face reaction to an involved question. Remember on Furlough Inmates could not partake of Alcohol or Drugs or get into ANY trouble. Tiny was not in any trouble at least not with the furlough rules. It was MOM he was in trouble with. Tiny admitted to back talking MOM. He never said why or what was said but Jamal had overheard. Jamal was still home from season break and grabbed Tiny before Mom's lightning left hook connected. This time it was Jamal's toned muscles that connected first.

Tiny did not go out on another furlough until he was sure Jamal was back at football pre-season training camp. Tiny learned many lessons from his Farm experience and furloughs. NO donuts, and don't ever back talk Mom especially when Jamal was home. There is always someone bigger and stronger. Tiny eventually healed-physically, and mentally and became more matured. He finished his 23 months and was discharged. The last I heard Tiny had gotten a steady job at Haber-dell Bakery and never again played stick-up at a Donut shop.

GARY SLUSHED THE WARDEN

Gary had a good job as a carpenter and an all around handyman. He worked long days, but not long enough. The problem Gary had was the Bar Room was too far away from his apartment. Gary had a few Beer's to relax and a few more to feel good then a few more because he couldn't feel it anymore. Gary was "wasted". He drove his Ford F150 pickup just a little to slow and kind of swerving. The police stopped him not far from the Bar. This was not Gary's first encounter with the police-maybe the 2nd or 3rd. Gary got all 23 months and he was lucky he got off easy.

The other officers and I were looking through the Inmate List trying to find eligible Inmates who were low risk for violence, escape etc. We needed good help and guys that had some kind of carpenter or work related skills. Gary's name popped up. He was here before doing weekends for his several DUI's. Gary did his first month in the jail "drying out". Lets give him a chance. I picked Gary up at the main jail and drove him to fresh air and the Farm. The Farm was an outside work program.

I took an immediate liking to Gary. He got along with everyone, had no hang-ups about discipline and always volunteered for any chore that needed to be done. Roofing, cement work, cutting grass etc. Gary was a model Inmate, not manipulating the system, not asking for any special favors-just doing his job. Gary was a great guy to have around and earned himself a special position in the Prison Garage washing vehicles and fixing lawn mowers.

Winter came and along with that came the snow and the Blizzard of '94. My telephone buzzed at 3am. I was being called in to work and plow snow. The usual 20 min. drive took an hour with the snow and white out conditions. Gary was already dressed, and charged up on caffeine-he was ready to go.

The heavy duty Chevy pickup had the plow and the full bed saltbox spreader topped off. I drove and Gary rode "shot Gun". He was my extra eyes, ice buster for the headlights and Windshield and with Gary's constant chatter would be company to keep me awake. I knew this was going to be a long night and day. We plowed for 24 hours stopping every couple of hours for a salt refill, and gas up. A couple of short naps and coffee kept us going. By the 2nd day the 30-inch snowstorm started moving out. I had to get all the snow moved off the parking lots before 1st shift change.

Gary hung in there like a real trooper—UNTIL. I was moving a little to fast and allowing the cement curbing to guide the plow blade. Absolutely perfect plan until the blade slipped, bounced up and swung the blade from left to right. The left side of the blade hit something solid-the cement curb of the storm drain. I never lost control when the Chevy Pickup did a double 360 left then hit another curb and a double 360 to the right. I had control-I held the wheel. I looked to my right-no Gary but I could hear him. Gary was on the floor kneeling facing the bench seat, his hands together in fervent prayer. Dear God, Dear God don't let me die-I never heard so many saints and Angels names spit out so fast in my life.

Finally the Chevy truck came to a stop. Gary crawled back on the seat. Nothing damaged, nothing dented-good. I said what kind of a "wuss" are you? All I needed to do now to finish up before 1st shift started coming in was the main entry road. Two long runs down and back the road and we would be done. The snowstorm was over and the sun coming up over the horizon started to make snow into slush fast.

Pushing slush is not easy especially if you do not want the slush to flow back on the road. I could pick up the speed now. A few hundred yards down the road was an open intersection and a clear view in all four directions. I had the Chevy in high gear, 50 miles an hour or better. Pushing slush fast in a high steady arc formed a rainbow in the morning sun and it was beautiful.

There was a stop sign ahead and Gary says go for it Nagster. Flying through the intersection I looked to my left and a four door black Buick sedan had stopped at the intersection sign. Somehow the plow blade switched from pushing right to pushing left and the arc of slush quickly covered the Buick and the driver who for some reason had rolled down the window. The Warden and his Buick were all slush and water.

Gary had a snide grin on his face. I knew I'd be in trouble now. I'm half way down the entrance road and radio procedure was broken. Command 1 to that S.O.B. and I knew he meant me and he was not happy. Command 1 to S.O.B report to my office ASAP. I said 10-4 out. The shit is going to hit the fan now. The warden was a former Marine major. Once a Marine always a Marine! Gary still had that strangely odd smile on his face. I dropped him off at the Farm House and I went to my execution.

Back inside the wire and walls I went to the office complex. The offices seemed deserted except for a few personnel who seemed deliberately pre-occupied. I didn't have to knock; the Warden was standing at his office doorway shaking slush out of his hair and clothes. Believe me you don't want to be standing at attention in front of the desk of a former Marine Major-especially the Warden. After an hour of being cussed out, chewed out and spit out with two layers of skin off my butt I was luckily back at the Farm House.

Early Friday afternoon could not come soon enough-Furloughs and then I could also go home. Gary got a special Furlough for working the extra time and about twelve other inmates on their regular scheduled Furloughs all left by 3:00pm. Sunday afternoon Gary comes back early swaying up the sidewalk to the front door carrying two cans of Budweiser still attached to the plastic molded six-pack carrier. Gary smelled like a brewery and some kind of strange smoke. Gary broke the furlough rules and we had to have him returned to the main jail.

As he was being processed back into the main jail all Gary was chanting was Nagster made me do it. Nagster made me do it. He said I got so upset and nervous I had to have something to calm me down. Word spreads fast in a jail and of course word got to the Warden. Again I'm standing at attention in the Wardens Dungeon. This time we're on a first name basis. The Warden added another nickname along with the first-Dip Shit and several other names I won't repeat.

To this day I still ponder just how the plow blade reversed direction so quickly and why Gary had that stupid grin on his face. Did Gary get even for scaring him so badly?

House Mouse

The FARM was an outside the prison walls work program. Thirty men mostly younger Inmates with non-violent charges could volunteer to work on the grounds surrounding the main Jail. They would learn about cutting grass, cleaning and raking out the wooded areas on the grounds, carpentry, mechanics and generally anything that needed to be done. This was a program to instil self-esteem and good work ethics.

All the Inmates lived in a three-story stone Colonial Farmhouse. The house comprised of six upper bedrooms with bunk beds, a kitchen and dining area, TV room two officers administration rooms and a basement for supplies, storage and the laundry.

Every house, any house has its usual resident mouse, at least one mouse. Halloween was coming soon and was an especially enjoyable time of year especially for the more fortunate guys who could go home for a weekend furlough. Before starting into the daily work routine as I was putting on my heavier field jacket I put my hands into the pockets. I near jumped out of my skin. Somehow a rubber mouse had found its way into my right pocket.

At the farm we worked but we also had some fun. Little pranks by both the Inmates and Officers made life more bearable. Humor is healing most of the time. My first reaction to the mouse was not a healing experience. The rubber mouse could have been a real mouse, a snake or something much worse.

I gained my composure. The house culprit or culprits were dead silent. No use to ask or react yet. I knew no one would "Rat" anyone out. The Officers, the three of us could and did stick together as well as the Inmates. I could feel the guys were waiting for a retaliation-a payback they knew could not be avoided. I watched who was watching me. I said to myself stay patient and make a plan. I plotted and in my head I planned my get even tactic to one or to all?

The morning of the third day was revenge day. My plan was to pick out one guy at a time. I already had my idea which of the Inmates could have had the most un-authorized access to the back office. The door was usually kept locked if an officer was not present. Sometimes an Officer would walk away from the office unattended. Trust only goes so far with an entire house of clowns or delinquents. With one Guy at a time I would have my revenge-my fun. The most suspicious guys I would save for last. By the third day the mouse had been almost forgotten-except by me. I had hid that rubber mouse so it could not come up missing until I had my revenge.

One day the mouse was hidden under the sheets of someone's bed. Another day it appeared in the clothes basket-a special treat for the already skittish laundry man Fernando. Another possible culprit could have been the houseman Joey. He cleaned, swept, mopped and dusted and would have had the easiest access to the officers clothing and gear. I had something special planned for him. I acquired another mouse-a squeaking mouse. The "house mouse" was hidden in the cleaning closet storage room inside the hanging broom. I hid behind a doorway when Joey entered the closet. I squeezed my special mouse. His reaction especially pleased me and was very effective.

Smoking was prohibited at the Prison or Prison Farm. Although the more clever and daring guys could get some smuggled in and hidden. I usually had an idea where hiding places were. I'd been around long enough I knew hiding places. Kenny the farm cook was the most ornery Inmate who was ever at the farm. Kenny could keep a straight face under any condition or situation. My main suspect for the House Mouse incident was Kenny. I was absolutely sure. The second panel ceiling to the far left. I pushed up the tile and low and behold a pack of Winston's. I made enough room in the pack to slip in the special mouse.

The scream of pure fear could be heard. I had caught Kenny dead to rights-a Bust. A Bust was a misconduct that would return the Inmate to the main Jail. But Kenny was the Cook and a good one at that. Good Cooks were hard to come by so I just gave Kenny a verbal reprimand. Not just for the mouse but also for the hidden cigarettes and the house mouse would remain a secret.

Every other week an exterminator came to the farm to spray around corners for bugs and vermin. One of the guys told the Exterminator about the house mouse problem. Extra traps were set. Those real sticky cardboard square ones were used. We were now prepared for a full-scale mouse invasion. I had caught the 'House Mouse" culprit but I wasn't done yet. Tiny our big guy on the farm-by big I mean 6'2" 300 lbs. Tiny could be compared to a baby elephant next to the size of the other guys. I called work out and everyone was on the move except Tiny. The metal armchair he was sitting on was or seemed to be fastened to him as he tried to sit up. Out came the House Mouse and I was holding it by the long tail and near enough to Tiny it was a get out do or die situation. Tiny was the biggest guy in the house and scared of a rubber mouse. Elephants are scared of mice also.

The last day of the House Mouse fun was coming to an end. The mouse I had hidden away for special occasions found its way into the Captains coat pocket. I thought the Old Captain was going to have a cardiac. When the shouting and swearing started in the office we all knew to keep quiet and with a straight face. That was the end of the "House Mouse".

The Salesman Floyd

Floyd was a salesman. Packets of the green stuff called Marijuana, and Baggies of the white stuff. Floyd owned his corner on Market Street. No one ever challenged Floyd for his street spot. Floyd had tough friends. Floyd was in Business for a long time considering he was selling an illegal speciality product. Salesmen Floyd had a good system. The person walking by on the street picked up the product and a partner down the street took the cash and gave no change. Floyd had it made and Floyd prospered. One of Floyd's buyers was an unkempt, longhaired, bearded, undercover Detective.

One sale, two sales and then the third sale was the magic number sale that done him in. Floyd had nothing to stand on. He could not claim entrapment because he was selling to a steady customer. Most of his other regular customers were also busted along with his partner. Floyd was "ratted out". The buyers got small time-Floyd got the whole 23 months with no good time. This was Floyd's first offence and he would be doing time. He was now a has been good salesman.

Floyd was now a resident in the Big Jail. With no behavior problems after 6 months Floyd became eligible for the Farm Work Program. The Farm was an old stone Colonial house with 30 men dived into 5 rooms. The land was One Hundred and Fifty acres of fields of grass-the legal kind of grass. All the Inmates wore orange uniforms for easy outside visibility. Floyd was tall and lanky and looked awkward in pants 6in short at the legs. Floyd pulled his white athletic socks up high to cover the difference.

As usual we teased. All the officers knew Inmate Court charges. Floyd had been a salesman. We put parsley leaves in one packet and Baking Powder in another and called Floyd into the office. I said Floyd is this the kind of stuff you sell? Floyd interested examined the packets and took a sniff and said no I don't sell that stuff go to the grocery store if you want that stuff. I said: "Floyd if I make one phone call to the "streets"? Floyd was horrified and most of the other Inmates were listening from across the hallway. Floyd said Nagster you are going to get me killed you wouldn't dare. The tuned in Inmates in the opposite room knew different. Nagster was different and I was unpredictable.

Floyd blended into the work routine and he said his sales days were over. He learned his lesson. Floyd was placed on the furlough rotation list, a cherished every second week two days home. He went out on his first Furlough back "on the Streets". The following Friday he checked out and came back to the farm Sunday on time. Floyd had fun this weekend. He made up for the money and the time he had lost. This time he just wasn't selling he was also using. Floyd used a little marijuana, a baggie of the white stuff, a couple of beers and a few uppers and downers. We call this a "cocktail". Enough to burn a hole in the small plastic pharmaceutical container each inmate had to test for when returning from furlough.

Wednesday was the day all the Laboratory tests came back from the Sunday night Bottles. Every inmate on furlough was forbidden to partake of drugs or alcohol and when returning was required to give a urine sample to check. We were working down over the hill cutting underbrush and raking- far from the Farmhouse. I was notified to bring Floyd in. I yelled over to Floyd that I needed to talk to him. Floyd knew he was busted-the criminal's sixth sense.

Floyd was not going back easy-Floyd ran. The cops call this resisting arrest and fleeing or something like that. I call it dam stupid. Where are you going to run in the middle of 150 acres wearing florescent orange? The officers on the Farm did not carry any weapons just handcuffs, a two way Radio, and diplomacy. I was not going to run after him. To my surprise Floyd jumped up and grabbed a low Maple Tree limb and climbed. A Maple Tree, with an eight-inch thick trunk about 40 feet high. Floyd was at least 25 feet up.

Swaying back and forth he was "flying me the Bird"-you'll never take me in. Fifteen Inmates all backed away and settled in to watch the show. How many guys were taking wagers on the outcome I'll never know. Floyd still swaying and "flying the Bird" looked like he was having fun. I had a situation here. This was my first Inmate in a tree that wouldn't come down situation.

Everyone knew the Nagster was 'crazy'', unpredictable and dangerous. I hollered back to Joe to go get me a chainsaw. I'm on the ground talking up the Maple tree but not to close unless the "bird" would start raining on me. I used all the diplomacy I could. Floyd was settled in for what he thought was the long haul.

I gave the required Direct Orders to get down out of the tree, the direct order must be stated two times. Floyd still swaying and "flying the Bird" the Husqvarna chainsaw arrived. Three pulls on the engine rope and the familiar Buzz started. Floyd yelled-Nagster you S.O.B you wouldn't dare. Always calm and collected especially when I'm about to do something sinister, two minutes later Floyd is riding the tree until both crashed to the ground. The Nagster is NUTS. Floyd mentally stunned from the change of affairs was hand cuffed and the Security Patrol that I had called for transported him inside the "Walls". Misconduct paperwork completed, the chainsaw part left out and Floyd back in the main jail I was glad for shift change.

Rumors spread in a jail real fast especially odd happenings and the Floyd up the tree and the tree cut down was a real good one. The words Nuts, Crazy, unpredictable were now interchangeable with Nagster and Respect. Don't mess with the Nagster.

Eventually Floyd was discharged. I made it a point to be there for his discharge. After all there were no bad feelings. I also had a hunch he would be back. The following day I was in Admissions picking up a new guy for the Farm and I heard a familiar voice. Nagster I'm back-take me to the Farm.

Floyd had faced the same Judge that had sentenced him 23 months ago. The day that Floyd was discharged, on the same spot and to the same undercover cop Floyd made his last sale for the next five years.

When marbles were given out-somehow Floyd was cheated.

AXE MAN and JACK

Jon was another one of those over eighteen's full of energy, ambition and determination. Jon was wandering around town late one evening. Not finding any of his usual friends he hung out with he found "Jack Daniels" and a long handle Axe. His determination mixed with the "Jack" was the beginning of a long lesson.

The police discovered him sleeping or most likely passed out on the ground next to a completely destroyed park picnic table and a hacked to death Elm tree. Still unconscious and handcuffed Jon was carted over to the police lockup. The next morning very much hung over Jon woke up fuzzy eyed looking through vertical Iron Bars at a short, stout middle-aged woman—MOM.

Mom already met with the police and read the damage report and Jon was fortunate he was in "protective custody". Drunk and disorderly, destruction of public property were the charges. A $21.50 fine and restitution for damages. This was the first time Jon got into any trouble with the law. Mom had connections. After the hearing all the damage assessments were paid except the $21.50. Mom said Jon was going to learn a lesson from "Jack"-a 90-day county time lesson.

At the prison Farm we were always watching the new

Admissions list for new men to replace those that had been discharged. This time a man was sent to us-Mom used her connections. Jon wasn't a violent offender or a runaway risk. Just keep him and his friend "Jack" separated.

The farm workers all lived outside the main jail in a stone colonial era farmhouse with 5 rooms upstairs each room had bunk beds and slept 6 men. Downstairs was a common room with a TV and a large dinning area and separate Kitchen and upstairs quarters for the 2 cooks. The farm was the perfect place for the first time offender.

Jon was a husky strong kid, a friendly easygoing guy. He got along with everyone and never complained. We, the few officers who worked at the farm usually knew each Inmates admission charges and that helped us to place the man in a certain job. Of course we found out about Jon's mother not paying the $21.50 fine. This was hilarious but we kept a straight face.

The first working day I pulled Jon aside and told him I had a special job for him. At the tool shed I managed to sort through and find a long handle axe-a very dull long handle axe. Everyone else were already cutting grass or raking. Jon stood by the tool shed with a full grin. Jon didn't like cutting grass very much but the axe in his hands felt good. Jon hadn't noticed the rounded edge of the shinny steel axe head.

I walked Jon to the edge of the woods where an old Elm tree stood dead for years. I said Jon we have to take this tree down, it's been an eye sore for years and the Warden wants it taken down. Jon said why not use a chain saw? I can use a chain saw real good. I said I hear you are real good with an axe. That big smile left Jon's face-he knew that I knew.

I figured that dead tree was at least a 90-day tree just enough time for Jon's lesson. I kept one eye on Jon and the other on the grass cutters. The grass cutting guys were all watching "Axe Man" and they were now the ones smiling. The Nagster had a victim. Like a spider with a fly caught in its web.

Slap thump, slap thump Jon was at it. Jon learned the thumps were ok but the slaps were a side step and duck or else. A dull axe does not work real well on dead wood especially an Elm. Day after day slap thump until at least a notch was starting to penetrate the wood.

Everyone at the farm had a nickname. Where they came from, what they looked like or how they carried themselves. Some came to jail already branded with a street nickname or a nickname from their last stretch with the County. Some nicknames came easy and some had to be pondered over and voted on. Nicknames are a guy thing or a jail thing and this was jail.

Jon earned his name the first day. Everyone agreed on Axe Man. All the guys had a calendar supplied by the Goodwill Societies that came to the prison on a regular basis. Each day a big X was placed on the calendar at the end of the workday. Axe Man scribbled his days in solid with black Ink blacking out the square. I've always wondered why.

Thirty days, Sixty days, this guy Axe Man was determined to drop that Elm Tree. Six handles later still slapping and thumping methodically working his way around the dead Elm tree there was definite progress. Axe Man cut completely around the tree trunk in an almost circle and all but two inches to go. Axe Man was getting impatient and I was getting nervous. Where will the tree fall? I'm not trying to kill this kid or me. A long rope solved the problem. As high as the rope could be thrown into the dead tree then the other end tied to another tree 30 feet away tied tight just in case. Axe Man said: Nagster you're a Bastard. Now I knew I was finally getting to him. Axe Man threw his axe down and started walking away. Is he leaving? Is he giving up?

Axe Man stopped turned around and stooped down like he was a tackle on a football team. He dug his feet in and screamed hike. My God. Axe Man attacked the tree full speed. Shouldering it again and again each time a crack sound and I could see the tree moving and the surrounding soil begin to give. Everyone stopped working to observe his bizarre behavior. On the last of at least 20 hikes I heard the final crack and the earth shake as the tree fell.

Did Axe Man learn his lesson or did I just oversee and condition a pathological tree killer? The last I heard Jon "Axe Man" was working for a Landscaping and Tree Trimming outfit. MOM paid the $21.50

Nicknames and "The Committee"

Pondering back over the years working in the Correctional field and blue-collar jobs, nicknames were a common and most times a fun activity. But at the Prison nicknames were essential and a vital means of identity—a serious and necessary consideration.

The Inmates at the Prison Farm were mostly younger guys that got mixed up in the wrong crowd. Guys with psychological problems; mostly undiagnosed conditions that led to erratic and at times bizarre behavior. Self-medicating on Street Drugs and or Alcohol led to trouble. These guys were not hardened criminals-at least I never felt they were criminals. They were just guys a little too ornery with a lot of energy who broke the established set of societies rules and the legal system slammed them. No pun intended. Society feels jail is the answer. The lock them up and throw away the key mentality.

The Farm Work Program was an extension of the main County Prison System. Thirty guys, Inmates that were considered non-violent and not escape risks lived away from the main Prison in a three story Colonial house. Job skills were practiced that the guys could put to use when they were finally discharged. Live, sleep, and work all at the Farm. Do what you're told and there would be no problems.

In a Jail environment Inmates thrived on giving out nicknames. The naming process became a "Committee" decision. All Inmates and Officers had nicknames. Some of the nicknames for Officers I won't mention-and an Inmate would not mention one within earshot. Everything was not all work. There were fun times after work. Basketball, Softball, Weight room, Television and time for pranks and jokes-good clean fun.

The Farm was not "us against them". I used to say one big happy family. On Sundays a non-workday I wore my Mr. Rogers button down side pocket sweater and would hum the Mr. Rogers TV show theme song. I didn't get the Mr. Rogers nickname. I was "The Nagster" because of my erratic driving skills. I most likely had some other names and that depended on what mood I was occasionally in. The Inmates had their laughs when the warden caught me driving crazy-to me it was not that funny. Nicknames defined the person. A nickname could stick to you for a long time-especially if that name was an especially irritating one. That name would be a constant tease.

Over the years there were a lot of different Officers and Inmates at the Farm, some just moved on, and some retired. Inmates were discharged and there was always someone to replace whomever. A constant rotation kept the Farm Program active. Many names I forget especially Sir names, first names I can sometimes remember-but nicknames I'll never forget. Funny nicknames, especially the funny names follow you a long time.

The first officer I remember only by his nickname; "Dog Hair". He got his name because he had a longhaired mixed breed dog that always slept on the officers' overcoat. Everyday he came to work his overcoat was covered with dog hair and on rainy days that was an unpleasant smell. One day "Dog Hair" was driving the ton and a half all-purpose Chevy truck to the County dump with two Inmates riding shotgun. A cigarette was tossed out the passenger side window. One of the open topped galvanized trashcans started to smolder. Looking through the rearview mirror "Dog Hair" noticed the smoke and fire and pulled off to the side of the highway.

Everyone got out of the truck to fight the fire. "Dog Hair" started beating the fire with his prized overcoat. Needless to say the cotton overcoat was destroyed-at least most of it. One of the Inmates was intelligent enough to reach behind the bench seat for a fire extinguisher. The fire was put out with the chemical powder. Word spreads fast in a small group. By the time "Dog Hair" returned to the prison farm he already had his new nickname-"Fire Dog". "Fire Dog" did not last much longer as an officer. He resigned when he was hired as a City Fireman.

Tony was already an older guy when he was hired as a farm officer. Tony previously worked in a steel plant until the collapse of that industry. Tony was a great guy and was looked up to by everyone as a grandfatherly figure. Tony was Italian and on weekends he would supervise the Kitchen Inmates. Tony's specialty was Macaroni. Tony loved Macaroni and Tony loved to eat! Except Tony was no large quantity cook and when you cooked for thirty guys at a time you had to know quantities and portions.

The kitchen pots were big, about the size of a four-gallon water bucket. Boxes of Macaroni came in twenty-pound Government surplus boxes. Since Macaroni was Tony's specialty both kitchen Inmates just stood back when Tony poured the entire twenty pounds of macaroni into the pot. Tony said that looks about right.

Kenny the cook, had to leave the kitchen before he would burst out laughing. The harder the water boiled the higher the macaroni bubbled to the top of the pot and over. The industrial size kitchen stove became a macaroni volcano. Was Tony in macaroni heaven? Macaroni covered the stove with the macaroni lava flowing on the floor. There still would be plenty left over for dinner. Tony's supervising the kitchen ended and Tony's nickname-"Macaroni" fit him just fine.

My nickname came at me early. "Nagster the Dragster" because of the erratic way I would drive and plow snow. Except when the Warden caught me and it wasn't so funny when he used that nickname with some time off to boot. I kept my nickname to this day.

Chuck was just "Big Chuck" for obvious reasons. Chuck was so big he was egg shaped. Chuck was so big when he sat in the wooden arm office chair and he got up the chair lifted with him. Chuck worked grave shift and his most important duty was an every half hour head count. Walk up three flights of stairs, count heads, and back down stairs write the head count in the log book and call into the main jail. I think the half hour call in was mostly to make sure Big Chuck made it back downstairs without having a Cardiac Arrest. Chuck's triglycerides were leveled out at 1100.

Another officer was "Stash"-he had an unusual mustache. Another became "Big Foot"-he wore a size 16 work boot and he could use it when needed. "Hat Trick" was another quick nickname for a nervous officer-he would continually flip his prison ball cap and catch it-"Hat Trick".

Official nicknames became a group effort. There was always a senior Farm Inmate Committee to either choose or approve a nickname. Nicknames either described or abbreviated a long and difficult Sir name and were much easier to remember. Sometimes a new Inmate would come to the Farm still carrying his "Street" nickname. These nicknames described his street activities or the crimes he was charged with. The "Committee" would approve this. The "Committee" had the last word on nicknames.

At this time I don't remember a lot of first names or even Sir names-but I do remember most nicknames. One guy only bought cupcakes for commissary-to this day he is known as "Cupcakes". One nickname he rebels about so naturally it stuck.

To this day I'll never forget Kenny. One of the best Inmates I ever had on the Farm. He came to the Farm at our special request because he spent five years "Up State" working in the kitchen. The big house as most inmates call State Prison. He was finishing his time with the County system. Kenny was also a big prankster and he knew all the "ropes". After spending all that time upstate you have to learn how to survive and Kenny survived.

Kenny's charges were attempted murder, reckless driving, intent to do harm etc. etc. Kenny was rehabilitated. His nickname followed him from State to County. Kenny was classified paranoid along with an anger issue. What first got him the State time was a Smith and Wesson revolver. His x-wife was riding along the freeway with her new boyfriend-they passed Kenny driving his old Ford 150 and flew him the "Bird" out of both the passenger and drivers windows. Now who wouldn't that piss off? Kenny was packing heat. Holding the wheel with his right hand Kenny aimed out the window with his left and let loose several rounds hitting the drivers door and cracking the rear window of the "Bird Finger Flyers". Two more shots blew out the back window as he ran over a bump in the road.

Click-empty-if I only had one more round. Police cruisers surrounded him from every direction. He surrendered without another incident. He was cuffed, booked and a no contest plea got him five years and 3 years probation. What Kenny said to the Judge-if I only had one more round. Kenny was lucky he missed his main target. Kenny's nickname-naturally became "Short Round". Kenny was lucky he was a lousy shot or we would have never had a murderer at the Farm.

Karl was a "real piece of work". Karl was not a criminal. Karl was a prankster and professional conman-one of the best before he was arrested. Karl was just Karl he had no nickname. Karl was a chain smoker-he loved his Salem's. When the Federal Government came up with a monetary reward for prisons who cut out smoking our County was one of the first in the Country to stop all smoking in the jail. The main prison was slowly one pod section at a time eliminating smoking. Karl was keeping count. Karl knew the Farm would be soon on the no smoking list. Karl started pack-ratting Salem's in every hiding place possible-like a squirrel hiding nuts.

Just a couple more weeks and his hell would begin. Karl was squirreling away Salem's not only for him self but he was planning a wholesale business at the farm. I'm good at finding hiding places. I had years of practice. I filled half a trash basket of contraband Salem's. Karl was going out of his mind. He told me I was destroying his inventory and livelihood.

One Sunday afternoon I was sitting in the office reading a Gurneys Catalog and Karl came into the office and asked to make an emergency phone call. I asked what was the emergency? Karl said he needed to call his mom and talk her into paying off his last County fine so he could be discharged. I agreed and Karl made his phone call. Karl was one of the best conmen I ever had contact with but his mother could play "tough love".

Karl's mom accepted the telephone call. In his most cunning, pleasant and convincing voice he begged his mom to pay the fine and she agreed. Now Karl was pushing the OH so nice con I will ever remember. MOM-one more favor. I just need a little money-walking money for when I get out. MOM asked how much? Karl said just maybe $500, or no more than $700 or a $1000 would last me a little longer.

Hello, Hello-MOM, MOM-silence. Karl spent another 3 months at the Farm smokeless. The Inmates across the hall from the office were listening-especially "The Committee". Karl finally had a nickname, a long and most unusual one unless you heard the phone call—Hello, Hello-MOM, MOM!

Like I mentioned: nicknames are earned and well thought out. Nicknames can follow you for a long time. Hello, MOM.

Donut Heist

Wednesday was always a special day especially this Wednesday morning. Haberdell Bakery delivers large bread racks of day old donuts-six dozen a rack-three times a week. Wednesday would be the last delivery for this week. A long holiday weekend coming up and a no delivery on Friday I will have to arrange a good plan to make sure we had enough donuts for the coming weekend.

If you don't spot a police car in the parking lot of a donut shop "monitoring" traffic; chances are 50/50 the cop is inside on a 10-2 call-the "john", coffee and donut stop. Correctional Officers are no different concerning the donut habit except the donut breaks are fewer. The jail officer is locked inside the walls and only could get donuts at the scheduled rotating chow break. Just the same the donut was special, an item worth waiting for. Maybe there should be a yearly donut award? The guy who can manage to sneak away the most times without getting caught award-the donut sneak award.

Outside jail officers have more freedom. I usually say jail officer because when I worked we were jail officers-today they are called Correctional Officers. At my jail we had an outside the wall program for the usually younger, not violent, less risk inmate. Nicknamed "The Farm" 30 inmates all stayed in a 3 story old Colonial stone house-6 rooms upstairs 5 men in a room with 3 bunk beds in each room. This was a comfortable arrangement at the farm and one that was not to be taken for granted. Screw-up, or any major behavior problem you were back behind the main jail.

Two fully armed Chevy Blazers with one officer in each one circle around the outside of the jail moving in opposite directions. Every now and then taking a long trip past the surrounding neighborhoods to assure the local residents they would be secure and safe in their homes. Security was tight inside and out with security cameras recording every movement-every possible escape route. Outside security took their breaks one at a time at the Farm House and that included the cherished donuts.

Inmates at the Farm did not always receive the donut rations, which meant the security officers did not either. A correctional officer as well as a cop could get real mean without that daily fix. Jail inmates and officers alike called the Farm inmates "cushion" inmates. Farm inmates had it good-except for the usual donut or two. I made sure a tray of donuts always made it to the Farm-legal or not I took care of all my guys. A tray of donuts held 6 dozen of the round powder, glazed, chocolate; cinnamon powdered or jelly donuts-all day old leftovers from the Haberdell bakery.

Tiny the Haberdell bakery deliveryman had been one of my inmates some years back. Tiny was now walking a straight line and a model law-abiding citizen. No donut protection routine. Tiny was a success story. Tiny got re-hooked on donuts as fast as he had been taken off donuts at the farm. As I said a well laid out plan had to be made. A no Friday donut delivery could be a disaster at the Farm so I had to do the big heist on Wednesday. I knew extra donut trays would be delivered to make up for the no Friday delivery. I usually "borrowed" only one rack of donuts every other day or so; that was easy to get slipped by on the Bill of Lading or overlooked. But this Heist had to be at least 2 trays or more; this could be difficult.

I rounded up the assault team. Plans were made. Plan A & plan B just in case. Security Officers, Tiny the Haberdell driver, Al-my other Farm officer and both kitchen inmates were "the assault team". Blazer 2 would hit the Haberdell Van on the way along the long entry road out of reach from the ever-moving security cameras; then deliver his tray to the opposite side of the House out of sight from the cameras. It didn't take a genius to get on to the timing of the cameras. Also there were some officers we called mouse, spider and stargazers. They would get bored at times and a few Security Cameras would get stuck either pointing straight up or strait down.

Plan A was a frontal assault. Directly opposite the last curve before the loading dock was a stretch of ground cover a mere 150 feet of open ground. I would call in a possible disturbance in the lower 50 acres. A tree covered mass of trees that could keep 4 cameras busy for at least 2 minutes in the opposite direction of our assault team-just long enough. Both Farm kitchen inmates and myself would lie in the high grass just at the edge of the sloping hill and when Tiny was getting near that last curve we would attack. Tiny had a regular 10am jail delivery schedule.

The Chevy Blazer's mission was accomplished. I got greedy. The donut syndrome got the best of me. I ordered plan B the ground assault. The donut Van was stopped; Tiny with hands in the air was prepared for the heist and opened the back cargo gate to the donut haul. Grab two racks of donuts and run as fast as 3 men carrying 2 trays of donuts could move 150 feet in less than 2 minutes. We got over and down the hill-all clear, mission accomplished.

Today was my unlucky day. Captain Barnes was manning the cameras. The regular camera operator had to take an early 10-2. Capt. Barnes was another former Marine that should have made General. Cap could use both hands and chew gum at the same time. Cap was good and Cap also had a 6th sense, which all Marines have. When I called in the supposed disturbance cap pulled 4 cameras to the lower 50 as I expected. I later found out I was deliberately being watched and under suspicion of being the donut thief. Captain Barnes zoomed in on me with a back fence Security Camera.

Back at the Farm House all of the assault team together again I unwrapped the plastic covering from the donut trays-donut heaven! Instead of the usual two-day-old stale hole in the middle donuts I had captured fresh wonderful glazed cinnamon buns-the real big kind, curlers, cream filled croissants, every kind of those special donuts I didn't even have a name for. Hero's, Billy, Kevin and I all heroes! We had captured the finest ever haul in Farm history.

My hand held portable transceiver barked "Command 1" to S.O.B. This had become my nickname to the Warden since the "Slushing" incident the past winter. Office telephone ASAP. I was DEAD, mortified, caught red handed and not a leg to stand on. Return all "Pastry immediately, report to the loading dock. Busted-Busted by Captain Barnes of all people. But how did the Warden get involved so quickly?

Two trays of donuts had to be returned-lost. Except the Warden used the word "Pastry". Command 1, Captain Barnes and Chef 1 the head Chef were all waiting for me at the loading dock. Why the big "welcoming party"-all three jail honchos together. I knew I was really in big trouble. The cussing and swearing started. The flapping and flailing of arms and all three were cussing and swearing. I'm not thinking what's the big deal-I would somehow have to save my butt and my job. Stay humble; keep my mouth shut-plead donut insanity?

A big reception was scheduled for all the County Judges, Commissioners, and Representatives. All of the Big Shots of the County would be there. The pastry was for the afternoon party. Any other day-just any other day but not today-this Wednesday WAS special. Busted and disgraced, the entire assault team rounded up for the ass chewing and possible firing squad. The Nagster-donut thief and the great donut heist of the Century all destroyed by one lone Security Camera.

The donut heist failed. We all barely kept our jobs-no one died in a firing squad, although WE--the assault team became one of the legends of the jail for many years. The "Andy Divine" story of the jail-"The Donut Heist".

BILLY

Billy was pushed through the school system after spending two years in each grade. Billy was disruptive, had a short attention span and was hyperactive. He was too much for the teachers to deal with or understand. Today we would call this ADHD. By the time Billy reached 8th grade he was 16 years old and quit school to everyone's relief. Working at several odd jobs of which none lasted very long Billy got married at a much to early age. He was immature and restless. The marriage did not last long. One day after an exceptionally trying day where he had an argument with the boss he was fired.

Billy ended up at the Pike Hotel and self medicated on alcohol. Someone started "pushing his buttons" and one thing led to another and bodies, tables, and chairs started flying out the windows and doorway. The barkeep dialed 911 and police cruisers started arriving in pairs. The Hotel was surrounded. Billy was oblivious to the police sirens and bullhorn. An alcohol-poisoned mind is a dangerous situation for both the afflicted and the police. Come out with your hands up barked the bullhorn. Billy only reacted to the noise and stepped through where the front door had been. Still holding a broken wooden chair he shouted "you won't take me alive".

The police would not shoot an unarmed drunk only holding pieces of a broken chair. One officer climbed the back roof only armed with handcuffs and pepper spray and moved into position at the front roof then dropped down on top of Billy. Temporally stunned he was handcuffed and the disturbance ended peacefully. Billy was slammed with enough charges to spend five years "up state". It all started because of a tough day and too much alcohol. Billy really had a bad day.

At the Big House Billy learned to read and write mostly by taking G.E.D. classes and taking Bible Correspondence Courses. He got a job in the kitchen and learned kitchen procedures and how to cook. A psychologist also helped with the "button" problem and other anger issues. Billy was transferred to the County system to finish his charges and make restitution for the damage to the Hotel.

Billy had been a model Inmate at the State without any violations or misconducts. He got a job in the County Jail in the kitchen. He had a good attitude and was still a model inmate without any misconduct. Billy was eligible for the Farm Program, we needed a spare cook and he would be our solution. The initial interview went well and he packed up his few belongings and I walked him out the Admissions door of the main County Prison.

The reason I know so much about Billy is because we spent so much time talking. I was mostly listening and Billy was pouring out his heart to someone he felt he could trust-someone he felt comfortable talking to. Billy became our spare cook and along with Kenny the main cook he was a good balance between Kenny the Clown and Prankster and Fernando our laundry man who still needed coaching. At least Billy was not a prankster so I thought-not at first.

Billy had not become over Institutionalized. He knew the ropes but did not use his long State time as some others did.

But no one got over on Billy and no one pushed him. They had heard about the bar clearing brawl and the police action. The farm guys were mostly younger guys who were 1st offenders and someone with much more experience could easily manipulate them. Billy did not manipulate.

Billy and Kenny stayed on the farm longer than any other inmates I can remember. I got to know both very well because they stayed in on weekends and we had more time to talk. They were not eligible for furloughs. To be eligible for furloughs there were two major obstacles. The first you had to have a place to go like a close relative without any firearms in the house and they could not be a former inmate. Second your sentencing Judge had to sign the original furlough order. Kenny's Judge had a good memory and remembered the last thing Kenny said when he was leaving the Court Room. If I only had one more round! No furloughs for Kenny. Billy did not have any crime free close relatives and the others would not take the responsibility.

The three of us became like brothers. Not brothers in crime just pranksters. Billy started to relax more since his up State time and Kenny felt he would be able to be trusted or let in on our little fun we occasionally had. The egg catch would be the first trial. Billy liked hard-boiled eggs and he was down in the basement helping Fernando with the laundry. I yelled Billy catch and I threw him a hard-boiled egg. Billy caught the egg and pealed the hard skin and ate it. I waited until I was sure he was finished. Again I yelled Billy catch it. This time I tossed a little higher and it was a raw egg-splat on his face and head. Billy took it all in stride. Yes he would be a good "partner in crime". We could let him in on some of our pranks. Kenny said just one more test-the bucket test. Two days later on a hot August day Billy was complaining how hot it was. I filled a scrub bucket of water and stood by the kitchen window just above the outside entry to the laundry room. I yelled Billy come outside the door, he did and Billy was no longer hot. Except I thought I heard a sound like S.O.B. Billy passed Kenny's prank endurance test and mine. He would never rat us out. Many more days were ahead and I was sure I would have some pranks taken out on me.

Hernandez

Hernandez was a quiet kind of guy who always seemed to be in deep thought or maybe just a little spacey. Hernandez was another guy who couldn't get anywhere near alcohol. But he was a good strong worker and we gave him the special job of truck man. Two inmates always rode shotgun with me in the Chevy Ton and a Half Truck. Extra muscle for the special jobs we were assigned to do. Once or twice a month we drove off the prison property and headed for the city twenty miles away to the Government surplus Warehouse. We picked up food supplies courtesy of the U.S. Government.

About a half mile from the prison Hernandez said he had to GO. Meaning he had to use a lavatory or a tree. No trees were in sight and Hernandez says there's a parking lot to your left. I pulled across the road and stopped at a parking lot to a Hotel and Bar Room. I said OK lets get it over with. This was his first time off prison property and did not realize I would have to be with him standing in the doorway. Patrons of the Hotel do not take kindly to a guy dressed all in orange entering their space. To most people Inmates are dangerous animals who belong behind bars. I don't feel that way but after so many years working with these guys to me their just normal guys paying for mistakes.

Hernandez got out of the truck and turned to me and asked for a dollar or two. I asked why would you need any money? Just in case I'm charged to use the toilet that's why. I got Hernandez back in the truck, turned around and headed back toward the prison. Hernandez caught me on a bad day and spent the rest of his jail time chopping wood and cutting grass.

Sam and the Sombrero

Sam was a Spanish American with a dry sense of humor and a determined responsibility. Sam was one of the few older Inmates who came to the Prison Farm. He soon earned a position cutting grass on the Toro riding mower. Sam was another guy who was sentenced to jail to "Dry Out". He didn't need a driver's license. Sam never learned to drive a car and he never tried. He received his 1st and 2nd D.U.I. riding a bicycle. He was not even on the road, he was trying to steer his way around a sidewalk full of people walking near the Court House. Sam had a bad luck day as luck goes, he nearly ran over the Judge who eventually sentenced him to the County Prison.

Sam was short and didn't weigh a Hundred pounds soaking wet. Sam had a big grin on his face when we taught him how to drive and maneuver the Toro. Sam's first weekend furlough he came back wearing a big multi colored 32" Mexican Sombrero. Most all of the guys at the farm wore ball caps with the beaks backward. We tolerated that but not the pants below the cheeks. Everyone had to pull the pants up or else. At the farm we were not allowing any street habits and rehabilitation was a must. Sam's Sombrero we made a special allowance for. This was a quite unusual head covering and probably the first worn at the farm.

Sam loved cutting grass with that Toro. Every once in a while as I did a drive by in the Chevy truck on the main entry road Sam was standing with Sombrero in hand scratching his head with the back flap up on the Toro. I would drive over and help him get the Toro started again. He said the Darn thing keeps shutting off. I was puzzled. The Toro was brand new and should not have any mechanical problems. After several days of this standing and head scratching I sent Sam to the Maintenance garage to check out the Toro. Nothing was wrong with the Toro so Sam was sent back to the field to cut again. Soon after he left the garage I notice Sam with Sombrero in hand scratching his head again.

I drove back up to Sam and considered checking Sam for flees, ticks or what ever. I noticed skip lines in the grass. An uneven cutting and it looked bad. Finally I called the garage supervisor out to the field and the stopped Toro. Big Foot, the garage supervisor came out with the Toro manual. Turning pages the answer hit him. The new Toro had a shutoff safety switch. If not enough weight was on the seat the motor would automatically shut off. Every time Sam hit a bump in the grass line he would bounce up and the motor would be killed out. Finally a solution was arranged. We fastened two fifty-pound dumb weights to the underside of the seat and Sam never had another stall out problem. He became the Butt of that story for a long time and we had to order two more fifty pound weights for the exercise room. I'll never forget Sam.

A.K.A. DELL

Dell was a big guy and I mean not fat big, but solid muscle big. Dell was one of the few Inmates who was eligible for the Farm Program with a block on his records. A block means no one except the highest Jail authorities could access those files. Dell most likely was not his real name. No questions asked I picked Dell up at the main jail in the Admissions area and together we drove back to the farm in the Chevy ton and a half.

After the usual signing in, clothing and bedding issued and a walk around the farmhouse to get oriented Dell wanted to start work. This was unusual for a new guy to actually ask to start working. But Dell was not the usual inmate. I drove Dell out to the woods where all the other guys were clearing brush, cutting small trees and moving stones. We were in an area where the John Deer Tractor couldn't penetrate.

Everyone noticed Dell get out of the truck but no one gave the usual wave or welcome to the Prison farm cheer. I'm starting to think again who is this guy? Dell started picking up stones and pulling the small trees out instead of the usual and deliberate waste time routine of dig and chop. One group of guys had been struggling with a big rock for several days. I'm using the work rock and not stone because this was a real big one. When enough dirt was tunneled around the rock I was going to have a long link chain slung around it and maybe the John Deer could drag it out of the woods.

Dell walked over to the rock and all the other guys backed off. He placed a hand on each side of the rock and with one pull he was standing holding the rock. This rock had to be almost 30 inches round on the average, and 18 inches thick. It had to weigh at least 300 lbs. Dell is standing there with this rock in his hands like it was normal to do something of this sort. He says where do you want it? All the other inmates are just staring and one of my few times I was speechless I just pointed to the edge of the clearing line.

This guy was strong and he absolutely deserved respect. Asking where do you want it was one of the few times Dell came close to speaking an entire sentence. Dell was quiet, a cold kind of quiet that I now realized he likely earned in the main jail and what ever his profession had been on the "streets" I did not want to know. Dell was different than the other guys at the farm and I could realize why the others were staying away from him-fear. Dell always kept to himself, never volunteered any information about his past, never smiled or even cracked a grin. He always had that hard stern look on his face as if he was buried deep within himself, pondering. He also carried himself with self-confidence and had no ego issues. I had never seen all these qualities in one inmate. I kept Dell as close to me as possible; I was concerned about the stern face and not intermingling with the other guys. Dell and I got along just fine. To me Dell was a gentle giant, a quiet stern faced giant.

I still wondered about Dell's street activities, wherever that had been. Was he transported to our County for "special reasons"? Dell started to slowly open up. Was Dell playing the tough guy role or was he the real deal? He didn't play softball or basketball with the other guys after work. He liked the weight room. He was only in the weight room one time. The bar bell weighed 35lbs. and all the weights were put on it. All the 50 pound ones were put on the bar. Dell curled it 3 times with one arm and set it down. I thought I noticed a grin or was it a grimace? Need more weights. I ordered another hundred pounds-not enough. At least I was getting some kind of response.

Dell had no recollection of days or time and was always asking if it was Wednesday yet. Wednesday was commissary night and Dell had one weakness, his Lorna Dune cookies. Dell would sit in the dining room and dunk his Lorna Dunes in a cup of milk. Dell was real serious about his cookies. Dell sat at his table in the dinning room, alone as usual with 4 packs of Lorna Dunes dunking one cookie at a time in a cup of milk.

A new kid was sent to the farm Wednesday afternoon. I don't even recall his name because he only spent one day on the farm program. The only way I can describe this kid is he was a smart-ass white kid with no common cense. Smart-ass walked over to the table where Dell was enjoying his Lorna Dunes alone, pulled out a chair, sat down and reached across the table and stole a cookie. With lightning precision Dell grabbed smart-asses wrist and said give it back. There was dead silence in the room and bodies started to move toward the far wall or out of the dining room. Inmates have a way of smelling trouble before it happened and this would be trouble. Smart-ass with his free hand stuck out the middle finger accompanied with the derogatory words. His last words for quite awhile. Dell reached under the table and grabbed the heavy iron cylinder that supported the table and with one fast movement smashed the table into smart-asses face. The living body was sprawled out on the floor covered in blood, blood splashed on the walls and ceiling. Before the jail goon squad arrived Dell was sitting on the floor finishing his Lorna Dunes and waiting for his escort back to the main jail.

Dell was dangerous-only when you messed with his cookies.
Dell was serious about his Lorna Dunes.

MEETING AT HIGH NOON

Steve and Mike came to jail about the same time. The local union had run into some legal difficulties. I can only say internal problems for obvious reasons. A lot of other guys from the same union also had problems. The best of the worst were Steve and Mike and they had a chance for the Farm Program and were accepted. I picked up the two lean and agile union guys at Admissions and we drove to the farm in the Chevy Ton and a half.

I handed out the usual Orange work clothes and mostly pink color bedding, then gave the usual walk through the Farm House and rules routine. The bedding was still all pink from the Fernando washing machine mix-up. I didn't want to have the white bedding all replaced at once. That would have caused too much paperwork and definitely a long explanation.

Steve and Mike were easy going and talkative except for telling me their exact court charges. I knew but let on I did not. Both guys were handy with plumbing, roofing, painting and just about anything that had to be repaired or replaced. In between the repair replace jobs they cut grass or ran the weed trimmers. The end of August is the worst time for catching poison Oak and poison Ivy. There is a difference and both can make you real miserable. Not many of us know if we are allergic to the Oak or Ivy until contact is made.

At the farm we usually had a lot of city kids who were never exposed to anything green or red and shiny. Every guy we had was working cutting grass and Steve and Mike were on the weed trimmers. Steve and Mike always did more than their share of work and started cutting up the tree trunks shaving the shiny stuff neat and clean. A stiff breeze was blowing in from the South directly into the mowing crew.

I came into work the next morning and everyone was pink! Pink calamine lotion was smeared on almost every guy in the house. Ten extra bottles were sent over to the farm for the epidemic. Steve and Mike took the worst hit from the wind and flying debris the day before.

Sunday was visiting day on the farm. Each Inmate could have two visitors at a time for one hour. A visitor had to have a clean record meaning they could not have been a former Inmate-anywhere. Visitors' records were checked carefully before the visit with the main jails computer system. Both Steve and Mike had a total of four visitors arrive at high noon. Signed in and the time written down they were escorted to the dining room where visits are held. Steve and Gary had pink smeared all over their faces and arms. A request was made to have two tables pulled together since they all knew each other. Steve said they were all friends and would just talk "shop".

Sitting in the office, with the echo usually coming from the dining room I could keep some kind of surveillance. Not much of an echo was coming from the visiting room. Mostly a lean close whisper and little could be heard visit. Odd? Usually a lot of noise would be echoing through. I had a double check done on the quiet visitors and nothing adverse came up except they were all in the same union. That was not against the rules. What ever was said or being planned I did not want to know. It was none of my business. Evidently Steve and Mike had respect, in and out of jail.

During visiting hours Earl came down the stairs from the 2nd floor only wearing his boxer shorts. Earl was a short Black kid and I have to admit before I "hid" him back upstairs it was funny him standing on the step landing all pink except for his eyes. Earl had poison real bad. Earl had little bumps, a sign of oak poison and he also was covered with the blistered rash, a sign of Ivy poison that had been scratched previous to the blisters. Calamine won't get rid of Oak poison. Only a steroid could help the Oak poison. Earl needed to go to the main jail medical for any prescriptions. Earl had to wait for visiting to end and shift change. And he would have to get clothes on-his regulation orange. Earl did not come back to the farm for at least a week. The bumps had gone away and most of the blisters but he still needed to use the calamine lotion.

I kept Earl out of the sun and away from the grass and poison for another week. Steve and Mike caught hell for trimming up the tree trunks. Most of the guys recovered from the pink epidemic. Some of the guys had to return to the jail and try again to get on the farm list especially after poison season.

TOP BUNK
BOTTOM BUNK
& ROOM 2

An Inmate working on the Farm Program was a privilege. The farm program was an out side the Main Jail work program. Inmates without serious or violent charges were eligible for the work program and the most attractive benefit was the every other weekend furlough. The farmhouse was a three story, stone whitewashed Colonial era house. The walk in basement was used for laundry and storage. The first floor had a kitchen, dining room, TV room and two rooms for offices. The second and third floors were used as bedrooms and one room for Lockers for daily use such as clothing, commissary and personal items.

A total of six bedrooms with three bunk beds in each could sleep thirty guys or more if needed. Most of the guys we had at the farm were younger inmates who should be separated from the hardened jail inmate. The reasoning was why expose a young guy to the tricks of the criminal trade. We experienced very few discipline problems-most of the time. The new guys always were assigned the top bunks and who ever slept on the top bunk automatically took the bottom bunk when someone was discharged. Most of the time this was an acceptable reward for the inmate who was on the farm longer. The farm had a lot of rules but all these rules slowly were added to as new situations were encountered.

A guy was coming over to the farm that came to jail as one of societies causalities. He received a jail sentence for being too tired to drive a bus but continued until he had an accident. This guy was an older guy and had no previous record. He was a good family man. He was slow moving and already showing his age. I felt he should receive a bottom bunk. Big Alvin had already moved to the bottom bunk. I knew I would have a problem coaxing him back up to the top bunk. I had a plan to remedy the situation.

Fernando had all ready asked to be returned to the jail because of his fear of "The Farm Louse". Dr. Bob had arranged a special cell in the medical section of the jail where Fernando's fear could be treated. Fernando, I had felt sorry for but in a way I was glad for his choice of protection from the "farm louse". I wouldn't have anymore-pink sheets or pillowcases and that included underwear and t-shirts. I had arranged for the older guy Peter to take over the Laundry job because I did not need any heart attacks while pushing a lawn mower. Just one more thing; I had to talk Alvin into the top bunk again and that would not be easy. My plan was to spread the word that Peter occasionally peed the bed. I had to make this seem real and a peed on threat to the guy on the bottom bunk. Carefully I filled a rubber surgical glove with water and some yellow food die. I tied the wrist part of the glove tight and placed it under Peter's top bunk on top of the sharp springs and under the mattress. The bunk beds were from the excess supply of WW II spring bottom type.

I waited and listened for the commotion. Alvin was in bed on the bottom bunk-already asleep. Peter climbed up the end of the bunk bed and crawled under his sheets and blankets. I heard the splash, yelling, and swearing from upstairs. Alvin was "pissed off" but I knew there would be not be an actual altercation. Alvin was easy going but he was serious about taking the bottom bunk until then. There was so much laughter coming from the upstairs all Alvin did was come down stairs to take a shower. I told Alvin I was serious about the old man and the peeing the bed problem. Alvin took the top bunk after I gave both the new dry bedding.

Howard also had a top bunk in room 2. Room 2 was my clown room. I always keep all the clown inmates in one room so when something happened I could easily yell at the entire group in the room, assign extra chores and I knew I got the right guy. No one ever ratted. Ratting is one of the jail rules they came to the farm with.

Howard was short and chubby with a stomach unbecoming a younger guy. Howard had a weakness-Corn Chips. On Wednesday night Howard always had delivered more corn chips than could be eaten in the dining room. The dining room was the only authorized room to consume food. Howard had to be sneak eating and I was determined to catch him. One Sunday during Visiting hours I did an extra head count. I always wore foam soled dress shoes on Sundays. I held my assortment of keys for a sneak entry. I heard the crunch ahead of time and was ready for the bust and usual extra work the Inmate would be assigned to do.

Howard was lying on his back, stomach towards the ceiling, with the blanket covering him from head to foot. An extra bulge sticking up from his stomach and caught red handed. Or I should say corn chip handed? The extra chore he received was moving a pile of bricks 12 layers high from one skid to a second skid and back again. I told him the reason was to sweep under each and make sure no beetles were nesting. There was always a cause and effect result, and no corn chips for one month.

Dickey Z

Dickey had a history of petty thefts, except he was not captured many of those times. The few times Dickey was caught he was smart enough to commit the theft in a larger County. A bigger County that comprised a major City is usually more lenient with a petty theft than a smaller County because of the city Jail overcrowding situation. Dickey always did small time. Usually he just did a few months jail time with a period of probation following him.

Dickeys last petty theft was his undoing-he was caught and arrested. He was running and a train was blocking his escape route. The train was moving slowly and Dickey caught a ride. He did not enter any of the passenger rail cars. He climbed to the top of the cars and maneuvered a final run to get just far enough from the cops where he could jump to freedom. Passenger cars near a city are connected on the top by a high voltage electric wire. Dickeys head touched a hot wire and he blew up. I mean he was zapped, shorted out falling off the train to the rough ground below. Dickey was down and out and he had fallen into another county-my County.

The cops called in an ambulance and the medics did as much as they could. He spent more than several months in a Hospital. A preliminary hearing was held at the hospital after dickey was put back together. The top of his head was fried, all hair burned off, multiple stitches on the top of his head, a glass eye and false teeth were enough so he could be transported to a jail infirmary. He also lost his left leg below the knee. A wooden leg and a toupee completed his blowing up run away attempt. Dickey learned a lesson about train cables and is the talk of many police departments to this day because he survived. At the hospital he wasn't rehabilitated, he was rebuilt and the electric zap must have scrambled his brain. His running and thievery were over. Dickeys new outlook on life was a 6x9 cement block cell.

Dickey slowly went through rehab at the prison and was able to walk, eat and talk again. Dickey knew he was fortunate to be alive. He also must have had a near death experience. He fit in with the other inmates in the main jail but his train near escape followed him. He was also an oddity with the other inmates. Dickey walked with a limp, always leaned his head toward the left when looking at someone and still talked with a slow forced verbal drawl. He earned a position in the jail kitchen and eventually up as a spare cook. As usual at the prison farm we always kept our eyes open for someone who could cook. "Zim Boom", as he was naturally nicknamed came to the Farm Program on a trial basis. We had to be sure he could manage the steps and be able to do enough work, especially in the kitchen to warrant his farm status. Zim was easy going, got along with everyone and somewhat of a prankster. Once in a while one of his arresting police officers stopped in at the farm just to visit the "survivor".

After a few weeks one of our cooks was discharged and Zim was made head cook. Zim was a good cook, always had the meals on time and the food was good considering he was using the Government Surplus supplies. Maybe Zim was given to much praise and the other farm inmates felt Zim was ready for some fun. I always arrived at work a half hour early, my shift started at 6am. The inmates were fed breakfast at 6am and one morning breakfast was late. Zim was never late with his meal schedule. I did not have to ask what the problem was, Zim told me first. Someone had stolen his wooden leg and getting down the stairs and working the kitchen propped up with a crutch under the left armpit had slowed him up.

About a week later like anyone else with false teeth Zim left his in a solution container overnight. Zims teeth went missing and it was Steak Sunday! His glass eye never went missing. Glass eyes to me are somewhat scary and I guess was also scary to all the other prankster guys at the Farm. We had a lot of good fun with Zim. When he was finally discharged the police department talked the passenger transportation company to give Zim a job as a Conductor. And this job was also on a trial basis. Zim had a great respect for passenger trains.

The Nagster